Original title:
Aspen Awakenings

Copyright © 2025 Creative Arts Management OÜ
All rights reserved.

Author: George Mercer
ISBN HARDBACK: 978-1-80567-003-2
ISBN PAPERBACK: 978-1-80567-083-4

A Symphony of Changing Colors

The leaves burst forth with vibrant hues,
Dancing like socks that lost their pairs.
A painter's whim, they choose to muse,
As squirrels chatter, free of cares.

They twirl and spin in breezy cheer,
Each gust a joke, each branch a stage.
Who knew trees had so much flair?
Nature's comedians, wise and sage.

Roots of Renewal

The roots are tickling soft, damp earth,
Throwing parties for worms and bugs.
A fungal rave, what a rebirth,
With mushrooms strutting out in shrugs.

The ground giggles, life wakes up,
As seedlings poke with happy grins.
A comedy of growth in a cup,
Where every spout's a chance to win.

Where Sunlight Meets the Silence

Beneath green canopies of laughter,
Sunbeams play hide and seek all day.
Shadows stretch, a playful banter,
While critters grin in a sunlit ballet.

The woods echo with bright delight,
As dappled light, like whispers, flows.
Each beam a jester, bold and bright,
Painting antics on the mossy rows.

The Spirit Beneath the Bark

In every tree, a spirit yearns,
With jokes tucked in the knotted grain.
As branches sway, the laughter churns,
Echoing through the woodsy lane.

Cracks and creaks, they pass the time,
Sharing tales of weathered years.
A giggle here, a playful rhyme,
These trees hold wisdom wrapped in cheers.

Harmonies of a New Dawn

Birds are singing songs off-key,
Making squirrels dance in glee.
Sunlight tickles the frosty floor,
Even shadows are too shy to snore.

Clouds are fluffier than my cat,
Trying to fit in a tiny hat.
The sun yawns wide, with golden light,
And trees laugh softly as they take flight.

Embracing the Chilly Embrace

Frosty noses, a comical sight,
Woolly hats worn very tight.
Hot cocoa spills as laughter flies,
While snowmen tell their snowy lies.

Gloves are mismatched, a grand parade,
As penguins slip in a nifty charade.
Everyone slips with a chuckle and cheer,
Wishing for warmth, but hey, we're here!

Enchanted Glades at Daybreak

Morning dew, like jewels, they gleam,
As rabbits hop into a dream.
A fox sneezes – oh what a sight!
The woods chuckle at the morning light.

Trees gossip about last night's dance,
Acorns chuckle at their chance.
Leaves twirl in a frolicsome spree,
While the sun joins with a warm decree.

The Thrum of Life Beneath Snow

Beneath the snow, the critters snore,
While winter plays the perfect score.
A mole hums a quirky tune,
And rabbits plot a spring monsoon.

Icicles dangle like silly teeth,
As winter's fun is underneath.
Life is jesting in a winter's cloak,
With whispers and chuckles, all under stoke.

Awakening Canopy

Beneath the leaves that dance and sway,
Squirrels gossip in their playful way.
A raccoon dons a leafy hat,
While the owls hoot, 'What's up with that?'

The branches stretch, they crack a grin,
As the sun rises, let the fun begin!
Birds in chorus sing a tune,
While chipmunks plot a nutty heist at noon.

Secrets Beneath the Quaking Boughs

Whispers of wind tell tales unknown,
As beetles play on a wooden throne.
A toad croaks jokes so ribbit-full,
While ants march like a tiny bull.

Underneath where shadows lie,
A raccoon jokes with a butterfly.
'Why do you flutter and never sit?'
'I'm just too pretty to commit!'

The First Light on Frosted Branches

Morning breaks with a cheeky wink,
Pine cones giggle and almost stink.
A rabbit hops in a frosty dance,
While frostbite squirrels try their chance.

Sunlight tickles the snowy ground,
As critters laugh, joy's all around.
Popcorn clouds in the bright blue sky,
And hey, is that a flying pie?

Dreams in the Shivering Shadows

In shadows where the giggles creep,
Bunnies plot while the pine trees sleep.
A fox in pajamas tells a tale,
Of a snail's race to mail a valentine's trail.

The underbrush bursts with sneaky glee,
While the butterflies sip on chamomile tea.
'This isn't a dream!' the critters all say,
'With friends like these, we simply must play!'

Ephemeral Moments of Rebirth

A squirrel in a tutu, what a sight,
Chasing his acorn in morning light.
Buds burst forth, all snug and tight,
While bees debate who starts the flight.

Worms in the soil, hold a parade,
With tiny hats, they're not afraid.
The sun peeks out, a playful charade,
Nature's spring antics, a grand upgrade.

Serendipity Among the Leaves

A bird sings loudly, thinks he's a star,
Mistakes a twig for his guitar.
Grass blades dance, they know who they are,
While butterflies drift, and giggle from afar.

The wind joins in with a playful tease,
Tickling branches, swaying with ease.
A rabbit hops, he's got the keys,
To secret spots where laughter frees.

Twilight's Gentle Farewell

Crickets gather, preparing for shows,
As fireflies flaunt their flashy clothes.
A raccoon sneaks, where mischief flows,
While shadows stretch, like sleepy toes.

The moon peeks out, with a cheeky grin,
Watching the day say goodbye, with a spin.
Stars twinkle, as if in a din,
Of stories told where laughter's been.

The Radiance of Awakening Colors

Daffodils giggle, up from their beds,
Donning bright hats for their tiny heads.
Colors burst forth, like paintball spreads,
While tulips wave for the fun that spreads.

Pansies sport bow ties, all in a row,
As the daisies dance with a sweet flow.
Nature's fashion show, don't you know?
Each petal has secrets that they can show.

Flutters in the Midst of Stillness

A flutter here and there, oh my!
A squirrel with bids to fly!
He leaps with grace, then takes a dive,
While onlookers giggle and strive.

Leaves shake and shimmy in the breeze,
A dance of sorts, if you please.
A bird stops in, strikes a pose,
Then off it goes, in feathered clothes.

The Pulse of Earth's Rebirth

Underfoot, worms wiggle and jibe,
Writing poetry in leafy tribe.
They speak of spring, the world awakes,
With every squirm, a joke it makes.

A tiny sprout, with all its might,
Wants to break free and join the sight.
"Hey, look at me!" it shouts so loud,
But winds reply, "You're still too proud!"

Whispers of Silver Leaves

Silver leaves giggle, rustle their tails,
Telling secrets to the rambling snails.
Each tale is wilder than the last,
Of summer dreams and winter's past.

A gust of wind takes off a hat,
Whirling 'round, oh what a spat!
Nature chuckles, the sun beams wide,
As hats collide, what a silly ride!

The Dance of Golden Branches

Golden branches sway and sway,
Joking with each other all day.
"Who can bend the lowest?" they jest,
"No one's as silly as the rest!"

They shout and twirl, and then they clap,
The birds join in, what a mishap!
With every twist and turn they make,
Laughter echoes for laughter's sake!

Nostalgia of the Northern Breeze

The wind whispers secrets, tickling the trees,
A squirrel with attitude, dancing with ease.
He wears a small acorn, his fanciest hat,
Chasing a chipmunk who's got quite the chat.

Pinecones are weapons in their silly fight,
Bouncing around like they're taking flight.
The laughter of leaves, how they shimmy and shake,
A breeze full of giggles, a nature's mistake.

Suddenly a bear comes stumbling along,
Tripping on roots, but he sings quite a song.
He's off to the river, with a splash and a dive,
Even the grumpy old moose feels alive!

The sun paints the scene, a bright golden hue,
While rabbits don waistcoats, in dapper debut.
With a chuckle, a wink, they greet the new day,
In the dance of the forest, come what may!

A Tapestry of Awakened Growth

Flowers in bloom wear their finest attire,
Bees buzzing loudly, a chorus of choir.
The daisies debate who's the brightest of all,
While the mushrooms sit giggling, much too small.

A frog in a bowtie leaps into the scene,
He croaks out a joke that's decidedly mean.
The toads roll their eyes with a cold, froggy glare,
"Ribbit, ribbit, buddy, we don't even care!"

Along comes a snail, with a shell made of gold,
Slowly but surely, he tells tales of old.
He boasts of the nights spent under the stars,
Rolling his eyes, saying, "They're just tiny cars!"

Grasshoppers cheer with a jump and a jig,
Waltzing in circles while eating a fig.
The sun dips low, closing a day full of cheer,
Nature's own laugh track rings bright and clear!

Melodies of the Forest Floor

The leafy refrain starts with rustles and cracks,
As critters parade with their shiny backpacks.
A raccoon in goggles is scouting for snacks,
While ants form a line with their picnic knapsacks.

A rhythm of laughter, a beat from a tree,
Owls hoot in harmony, sounding so free.
The twigs tap along like they've found their own groove,
In this forest of boogie, it's impossible to move!

A hedgehog in shades, oh, what a sight!
Dreaming of disco under the moonlight.
He rolls with a swagger, a charm all his own,
"Just wait for my moves; I'll shake up this zone!"

The night hums a tune full of giggles and glee,
As shadows perform, just as sprightly as me.
With each playful rustle and delightful refrain,
The forest is dancing, nothing is plain!

The Resurgence of Nature's Brush

A painter arrived with a laugh and a grin,
Spilling bright colors all over the skin.
The leaves shake their heads, covered in paint,
"Who knew a tree trunk could look like a saint?"

A palette of blossoms emerges with flair,
Beehives in chorus, sweet melodies share.
The dandelions chuckle, their fluff in the wind,
While flowers are squabbling over who's trimmed!

The sun paints the sky with a splash of bright gold,
And the critters convene, new stories unfold.
Even old rocks have a story to tell,
They sit and they wish, "Oh, to dance very well!"

With each stroke of brilliance, the woods come alive,
A humorous world where all critters thrive.
So join in the laughter, as nature conspires,
To fill up the universe with joy and desires!

Flutters of Change in the Air

The leaves start to giggle, a flutter of green,
As squirrels play tag in the spaces between.
With each gentle breeze, they dance and they sway,
While trees chuckle softly, 'It's time for some play.'

A chipmunk winks, it's wearing a hat,
Saying, 'Winter's gone, and how about that?
With skies turning blue, let's throw a parade,
All creatures take part, no need to be paid.'

Birds chirp in rhythm, a silly old tune,
They drop hints of mischief 'neath the bright moon.
The flowers break out in a colorful laugh,
As bees take a bow, in nature's big staff.

Seasons of Promise Beneath the Canopy

Beneath the tall trees, the chatter begins,
With worms pulling pranks, as bright as their skins.
Each blossom whispers secrets of spring,
While bugs don their shades, oh, the joy that they bring!

A hiccuping brook giggles along,
Joining in harmony, hums a sweet song.
The sun throws confetti from morning till night,
As geese wear their socks, oh what a sight!

With vines in a frenzy, they twist and they twirl,
And mushrooms pop up for an unexpected swirl.
Nature's a circus, with joy all around,
As laughter and wonder together abound.

Emerging from Winter's Embrace

From blankets of snow, a brave flower peeks,
With a wink and a nod, it giggles and squeaks.
The sunlight arrives, in a bright, sassy mood,
While icicles chuckle, all frozen and rude.

A weary old bear stretches out with a yawn,
Saying, 'Winter, you stinker, I'm ready for dawn!'
Grass blades are schmoozing, they pop their heads up,
As bunnies declare, 'Time for a hop and a sup!'

The winds play tricks with the last of the frost,
While creatures just dance, never caring of cost.
The season of fun, with quirks everywhere,
As winter gives way, with a fanciful flare.

Life's Evidence in Nature's Heart

In the thicket of life, mischief is rife,
From giggling groundhogs, to sparrows' new life.
Each twig holds a tale, each petal a joke,
As laughter erupts, like the roar of a bloke.

The deer try to shine, with fashion so bold,
Sporting new antlers, oh so glossy and gold.
While raccoons throw parties, in moonlit delight,
They dance like clowns, under stars shining bright.

A parade of odd creatures, all winking about,
Each step is a giggle, from far and from out.
Life in the forest, an endless buffet,
Where humor and growth are just part of the play.

The Lament of the Withering Leaves

Oh, the trees are whispering, tapping their toes,
As leaves drop slowly, making quite the show.
They grumble and mumble, "We're losing our stash,"
While squirrels giggle, in their nutty dash.

Once vibrant and green, now a crunchy parade,
Each gust of wind gives their shuffling a grade.
With wistful regret, they wave to the sky,
"We liked being leafy, oh me, oh my!"

In piles they conspire, to plot their grand fate,
"Let's team with the dust, we can't be late!"
They frolic in circles, with a whirlwind cheer,
Bids farewell to the branches, nature's premiere.

Yet fear not, dear friend, for next spring's delight,
Will bring back a party, oh what a sight!
The trees will be lively, a full-on ballet,
While leaves learn to dance in their green cabaret.

Glen of Glistening Revelations

In the glen, giggles bubble, high and bright,
As blossoms come bursting, catching the light.
Butterflies giggle, with wings all aglow,
While llamas nearby start stealing the show.

Sunshine tickles flowers, they sway and they bend,
Like they're doing yoga, just around the bend.
"Namaste, dear daisies, rise up mighty tall!"
The croaking frogs join in, showing off their call.

With each gentle breeze, laughter fills the air,
As chubby bumblebees spin without a care.
"We're the reigning champs of this pollen ballet!"
They chatter about snacks, not a moment delayed.

In this funny glen, nature's humor prevails,
With chatter and chuckles heard through winding trails.
So let yourself giggle, let worries take flight,
For laughter and blooms share the ultimate light.

Beneath the Crust of Winter's Veil

Beneath the snow blanket, the mischief will stir,
As creatures plot pizza in the frozen fur.
The rabbits are dreaming of springtime delights,
While the hedgehogs roll mats for their comedy nights.

The icicles glisten, like teeth all agape,
As squirrels hold debates on the best winter shape.
"Let's build us a snowman," they conspire with glee,
And the snowflakes all giggle, in flurries set free.

The cold grips the glen, yet jokes still abound,
With snowball ammunition hidden all around.
A friendly white war, a laugh-filled display,
As citizens gather to play and to sway.

Though frost creeps aplenty, and stillness seems loud,
The critters find laughter beneath winter's shroud.
For even in snow, life finds ways to evolve,
With chuckles and warmth, all problems resolve!

A Canvas Painted in Green Whispers

On this canvas of green, the colors conspire,
Each leaf has a story, each bud's a liar.
The grass claims it's taller, the daisies say, "Oh!"
While the dandelions snicker, "We're just here to grow!"

The sunbeams chuckle, warming the scene,
As the branches exchange plots—oh, what they mean!
"A game of hide and seek, let's challenge the light,"
With shadows rejoicing, they dance out of sight.

In this quirky green haven, laughter takes flight,
With critters debating who's fastest in fright.
The turtles are slow, but they take the lead,
While the rabbits are hop-skipping, just full of speed!

Oh, a canvas of whispers, a gallery grand,
Where nature displays humor across this fine land.
So let laughter bloom between petals and breeze,
As we cherish the moments that tickle with ease.

Horizons of Hope in the Wilderness

In the woods where squirrels prance,
I lost my hat, it didn't stand a chance.
A deer cropped grass, gave me a glance,
As I chased my cap, doing a funny dance.

With pine trees whispering gentle jokes,
The birds laugh out loud, or maybe just croaks.
I crack a smile with all of these folks,
Who knew nature had such silly pokes?

The wildflowers giggle, swaying with grace,
While I tumble 'round, give the ground a kiss face.
A chipmunk winks, what a cozy place,
In this laughter-filled, green, wild embrace.

Nature can be a big comic show,
From the chipmunks' pranks, to the winds that blow.
I find my joy in this landscape's glow,
In the heart of the wild, my spirit will grow.

Lives Intertwined in the Canopy

Above the ground, the treetops play,
With branches that twist in a funny ballet.
Squirrels drop acorns, what a wild array,
While in the shade, I sit and survey.

The birds chime in with a raucous beat,
Conducting the trees in a symphonic feat.
A raccoon's mischief can't be discreet,
As he sneaks by, just to steal a treat.

A sunbeam slips through the leaves to peek,
Laughing at moments, so joyous, so meek.
At sunset, I trip, and it's not at all chic,
Yet in this ruckus, my heart feels unique.

Glancing up, I see a squirrel's grin,
He knows the best in a world so thin.
In laughter and light, we all fit in,
Intertwined lives, where the joy begins.

The Awakening Mosaic of Nature

Morning arrives with a vibrant spree,
Nature's palette shines for all to see.
A frog in a pond croaks, "Come join me!"
As I slip on mud, oh what glee!

The sun peeks out, painting skies bright,
While the ants march, what a comical sight.
One stumbles and falls, feeling light,
In this mosaic, everything feels just right.

Flowers bloom with a flourish and flair,
Balleting petals dance light in the air.
A breeze tickles softly, with love and care,
Nature's chorus sings, beyond compare.

Laughter ripples through rustling leaves,
Whispering secrets that nature weaves.
In this grand tale, my heart believes,
Even clumsy frogs can achieve their dreams!

Golden Tendrils of Life

In golden light, the ferns do sway,
While I trip over roots on my way.
A rabbit jumps out, in grand array,
We both laugh hard, what a crazy day!

Sunshine spills down like syrupy gold,
Nature's stories delightfully told.
A lizard does yoga, looking so bold,
As flowers bloom, so lively and old.

With each silly moment, my worries erase,
The forest's charm, a whimsical place.
Even the bees have their own little race,
Dancing on blooms, in a sweet, funny space.

In this tapestry, we find our way,
With laughter and wonder, come what may.
Life twirls and giggles, in bright disarray,
I cherish each moment, and joy holds sway.

Whispers of the Golden Grove

In the grove where laughter blooms,
Squirrels plot their nutty dooms.
Trees exchange their gossipy tales,
As dandelion fluff rides the gales.

Sunlight winks through golden crowns,
While mushrooms wear their silly frowns.
Breezes tickle a bark-clad back,
Nature's giggles spill with a crack.

Under branches, shadows play,
A deer yawns, then struts away.
With acorns marked as treasure maps,
The forest dances, perhaps with claps.

So come, join the woodland's jest,
The rustling leaves surely know best.
In this realm where laughter flows,
The secrets of the grove, everyone knows.

Echoes of Autumn's Breath

Leaves tumble down like clumsy fools,
They'll never win at graceful schools.
A crow caws out, a jesting prank,
His wings flapping like a spunky tank.

Pumpkins grin with toothy cheer,
While critters scurry without fear.
Rabbits boast of carrot quests,
While owls declare they know the best.

Snap! A twig sings out like a joke,
As a porcupine starts to poke.
Nutty puns float on crisping air,
With every gust, it's beyond compare.

In this season of colorful frights,
Nature's comic plays through the nights.
So grab a leaf and join the jest,
Where autumn smiles and plays at best.

The Dance of Trembling Leaves

Leaves hoot and howl, in rhythmic calls,
As breezes pull them into brawls.
Dancing high in shades of gold,
Their swaying moves are quite bold.

Acorns tumble, ready to roll,
While wise old oaks maintain their pole.
A clumsy raccoon joins the scene,
Tripping over roots, oh, what a queen!

Branches sway to a lively beat,
While critters scamper on tiny feet.
The forest floor is laughing loud,
With every twirl, it feels so proud.

Nature's disco, with sounds so sweet,
A woodland party that can't be beat.
So sway with joy amidst the trees,
And dance away with utmost ease.

Revelations in the Forest's Heart

In the heart where secrets dwell,
A chipmunk whispers, 'Oh, what the hell?'
With nutty wisdom, he shares his plan,
To host a feast for each little fan.

Moss wears slippers, all fuzzy and bright,
As mushrooms gather for a playful fright.
A fox juggles apples, quite out of line,
While a wise old owl sips on pine wine.

Branches gossip about the skies,
While shadows giggle, covered in lies.
With sunlight beams, they play peek-a-boo,
Crafting moments that feel like new.

So wander deep where laughter stirs,
Amidst the trees, where each heart purrs.
For in this realm, with whimsy wrought,
Lies a magic that can't be bought.

Nature's Gracious Invitation

The trees are buzzing, oh what a sight,
A squirrel's dancing, like a silly kite.
Birds are gossiping in a feathery choir,
While ants throw a party, dragging leaves like squire.

Frogs in tuxedos leap with great flair,
Chasing after flies, without a care.
Flowers are gossiping, colors in bloom,
Inviting us all for a jam in the room.

Bunnies with bowties munch on sweet grass,
While bees wear sunglasses, buzzing en masse.
Nature's a circus, with fun at its core,
Come join in the laughter, who could want more?

So grab your shorts and skip out the door,
The woods are alive, it's laughter galore!
Nature is calling, it's hard to resist,
Join in the frolic—just don't get missed!

The Glistening Dance of New Life

Little sprouts popping from the earth's warm embrace,
Wiggly worms join in a squiggly race.
Sunlight tickles leaves, making them giggle,
As raindrops tap dance, hopping with wiggles.

Butterflies float by, in a colorful spree,
Picking up gossip from the old maple tree.
Clouds overhead play peekaboo games,
While rocks tell stories with dignified names.

Daffodils twirl in their yellow-best clothes,
While daisies just lounge, getting all the doze.
The wind tells a joke, and trees shake with mirth,
As laughter erupts from the heart of the earth.

Nature's a party; come one, come all!
With giggles and wiggles, we'll have a ball!
So dance with the daisies and laugh in the rain,
In this world of delight, there's nothing to gain.

Harmonizing with the Elements

The sun sings boldly, a bright serenade,
While breezes pirouette, a gentle cascade.
Clouds drum along, a fluffy parade,
As mountains hum softly, their wisdom displayed.

Rivers are whispering tunes of the past,
While pebbles join in with a rhythm amassed.
The earth keeps a beat that we all can embrace,
Let's groove with the flowers, in this joyful space.

Raindrops clap hands, an applause so unique,
As puddles reflect all the laughter they seek.
Nature's orchestra plays a fantastic show,
Where every creature joins in, basking in glow.

Come dance with the elements, shake off your shoes,
Give in to the rhythm; you've got nothing to lose!
With smiles all around and fun we can claim,
Let's join in the harmony, never feel shame!

Emerald Symphony of Growth

Sprouts are sprouting, in a crazy spree,
With leafy coconuts, hanging from trees.
Vegetables chuckle, oh what a sight,
As radishes race, in the warm sunlight.

The sun plays conductor, with rays in full swing,
While bugs start to cha-cha, giving their bling.
To the rhythm of nature, so lively and bold,
It's an emerald symphony, a tale to be told.

Roots play the bass, shaking deep in the ground,
As blossoms all guffaw, twirling around.
A chorus of critters joins in the refrain,
Celebrating growth, it's sunshine and rain.

So gather around, let's join in the cheer,
In this garden of giggles, there's nothing to fear.
With joy in our hearts and laughter in tow,
Let's celebrate growth; let our spirits glow!

Echoes Through Verdant Valleys

The trees shake hands with the breeze,
Squirrels argue who's the best tease.
Birds compete in a morning song,
While deer crash a picnic, oh so wrong.

A rabbit hops in disco shoes,
While ants march on with tipsy blues.
The sun yawns wide, it's time to play,
As grass tickles feet in a silly way.

Frogs join in with a leap and splash,
While owls hoot and giggle in a bash.
The brook chuckles along its route,
As nature throws a wacky shout-out.

In valleys rich where laughter roams,
Tall tales are spun among the homes.
Echoes weave through the lively space,
In this wild and whimsically funny place.

Nature's Awakening Gaze

A daisy winks, its petals bright,
A bumblebee wears shades, what a sight!
Mice gather round in a tiny rave,
Dancing with mushrooms, oh how they crave.

Morning dew's a sliding board,
For frogs who leap, and won't get bored.
The wind whispers jokes to the trees,
While snails move at a pace that's a tease.

Clouds drift by, with shapes so odd,
A cat? A hat? Oh, that's a nod!
Each leaf rustles with giggles galore,
Nature's trying stand-up, who could ask for more?

A parade of creatures line up to vie,
For the crown of the funniest, oh me, oh my!
Laughter echoes in this vibrant haze,
As nature gives us its funny gaze.

Beneath the Canopy's Caress

Under the leaves, shadows play,
Where squirrels sneak snacks in a charming way.
A woodpecker's knock turns into a beat,
And tree trunks bounce to a forest retreat.

Moss stretches out, wearing a grin,
While lizards strut, with a flash and a spin.
A raccoon pops in, wearing a mask,
For hidden snacks, it's quite the task.

Sunbeams peek through, playing hide and seek,
The butterflies flit, oh what a cheek!
With giggles and sighs, the branches sway,
In nature's embrace, we laugh and play.

A chorus of chuckles from creatures abound,
In a kingdom where silliness knows no bound.
Beneath the canopy's whimsical dress,
Life thrives in laughter and pure happiness.

Forest Dreams in Morning Light

In morning light, the forest wakes,
With sleepy branches and playful flakes.
A bear on a yoga mat tries to pose,
While startled birds flutter from their doze.

The sun spills giggles across the ground,
While bushes gossip without a sound.
A fox prances in mismatched socks,
Thinking it's cool to flaunt those rocks.

Laughter bubbles in every stream,
As fish practice their latest meme.
The wind joins in with a cheeky twist,
Playful nudges that can't be missed.

Dreams in the forest are wild and bright,
With fun galore in the morning light.
Where every rustle and every cheer,
Brings magic to life and fun so dear.

The Quiet Return of Life

In the springtime's cheerful glow,
Bunnies hop and squirrels throw.
A bear decided to take a stroll,
He tripped on roots and lost control.

The flowers wear their colors bright,
A bee buzzes in sheer delight.
A snail slides by, so very slow,
At this rate, he'll miss the show!

The trees start shaking off their sleep,
As frogs croak songs that make you leap.
They form a band and start to play,
But oh! That frog forgot his way!

With every chirp and every rustle,
The woods come back, and oh, the bustle!
Nature laughs, and we can see,
This wildness brings such joy and glee!

Brushstrokes of Morning Mists

Morning mists in swirling dance,
A clumsy deer gives it a chance.
He trips and tumbles through the haze,
While robins chirp their morning phrase.

The painter's brush in nature's hand,
Colors spill across the land.
A raccoon shows up, sly and bold,
Painting paw prints on the gold.

Ducks quack loudly, full of cheer,
As they make their grand debut here.
One takes a leap, then makes a splash,
And all the rest just giggle and clash.

The mist rolls back, the sun breaks free,
And nature's laughter calls to me.
Through brushstrokes bold, a day unfolds,
In scenes of humor, stories told!

Nature's Gentle Rebirth

Little sprouts peek from the ground,
While worms create their wriggly round.
A caterpillar munches with glee,
"Keep chewing, and soon you'll be free!"

The sun shines down, a warming glow,
As flower petals start to show.
A busy ant, with his grand plan,
Carries a crumb, oh, what a span!

In the pond, the frogs begin to sing,
But one frog's voice is just a fling.
He croaks a note that sounds quite wrong,
The others laugh and sing along.

Nature wakes, all fresh and bright,
It's a funny, quirky sight!
With every giggle, wiggle, and fun,
A silly world where laughs have begun!

The Call of the Awakening Woods

In the woods where laughter rings,
A squirrel tries his acorn flings.
He aims to land it 'just so right,'
But hits a branch—oh what a sight!

The wind whispers, "Come outside!"
As leaves dance in a silly glide.
A woodpecker drums a beat,
But rhythm's off—he's lost his seat!

Sunbeams tickle, warming all,
While creatures gather for the call.
A hedgehog rolls and strikes a pose,
"Oh dear! Is this how fashion goes?"

The woods awake in humor's grace,
With smiles dancing on each face.
In this adventure, loud and bold,
Nature's laughter never gets old!

The Awakening of Earthly Dreams

In springtime's dance, the flowers cheer,
Dandelions dress like they own the sphere.
Bees buzz in a comical race,
While ants hold tiny, impromptu base.

Raindrops tap like a drummer's beat,
On rooftops, oh what a funny feat!
Nature's joke, waiting on a tease,
As squirrels attempt to climb with ease.

The grass all laughs with a gentle wave,
Tickled by winds, it's party time, brave!
Worms wear sunglasses in cheeky style,
Underground parties, they're there for a while.

As colors burst and shapes collide,
Life wakes up on a joyful ride.
Nature's giggles echo through the trees,
As creatures join in the symphonies with ease.

Kaleidoscope of Silent Births

A butterfly's sneeze sends colors ablaze,
A dandelion's giggle in sunlight's gaze.
Crickets chirp jokes in a rhythmic spree,
While the pond fun hosts fish fancy tea.

The trees wear hats on their leafy crowns,
While rabbits hop, adorned in frowns.
Every twig is a bard, sharing a laugh,
As worms tell tales, all silly and daft.

Flowers blink at the sun's bright smile,
Their petals bright, they flaunt in style.
A snail rehearses its slow-motion race,
While frogs in the pond practice their bass.

In this landscape rich with quiet fun,
Life bursts forth, rejoice everyone!
In hues so vivid, in moods so spry,
Nature wears a sparkly, cheeky tie.

Beneath the Shimmering Sky

Clouds wear pajamas, fluffy and wide,
As hedgehogs roll down the hill with pride.
The sun throws confetti, a golden spree,
While shadows play hide and seek with glee.

The wind mimics voices, a comedic chat,
Whispers of chortles as squirrels cavort,
The streams giggle softly, a playful muse,
As daisies don hats in quirky hues.

A bird croons a tune that's silly and bright,
While frogs leap about in joyous flight.
As the breeze holds its belly with laughs,
The world spins on whims, embracing the gaffs.

Night falls gently, like a cozy sock,
The moon winks playfully, around the clock.
Beneath the shimmer, joy takes its pledge,
As starlit sprites dance on a delicate ledge.

Groves of Awakening Whispers

In the grove where whispers weave and waltz,
Trees share secrets without any faults.
Birds crack jokes on the wind's soft breath,
While crickets chirp like there's no death.

A raccoon conducts with a leaf in paw,
To a concert where bumblebees find their flaw.
Nature's symphony, a careful prank,
Leaves flutter down like they're in a tank.

Around the brook, laughter spills like wine,
As frogs put on capes — it's hero time!
Daisies giggle as they twist and twine,
Opening up, they sip sunlight fine.

In groves that whisper of capers rare,
Join in the jest, throw away despair!
With roots of laughter and trunks so bright,
Nature celebrates its neighborly plight.

Swaying in Soft Sunlight

Bouncing branches in the breeze,
Leaves giggle, just like me.
Squirrels dance in crazy loops,
Shaking hands with leafy troops.

Sunbeams play tag in the trees,
Tickling bark with playful ease.
A tree stump jokes, "Can you believe?"
Together we laugh, none to grieve.

Clouds are sheep, drifting so wide,
With dreams of mischief, they glide.
A bee buzzes, doing a jig,
While ants march, wearing hats big.

Nature's circus, full of cheer,
Making every moment dear.
Join the fun, let's prance about,
Under sunlight, without a doubt!

Unfurling in the Daybreak Glow

Petals stretch, a sleepy sigh,
Winking daisies say goodbye.
Morning coffee spills on dew,
The sun laughs as it shines anew.

Birds bring breakfast with their song,
As crickets cheer, all day long.
Butterflies wear silly hats,
While flowers speak in funny spats.

A snail races, but takes a nap,
It dreams of winning, what a chap!
The garden hums in joyous jest,
With all this laughter, who needs rest?

Blossoms burst with vibrant flair,
Tickled pink, they dance in air.
A jester bee buzzes around,
Spreading laughter all around!

Melodies of Morning Reverie

Chirps and giggles fill the air,
Nuts are cracking with great flair.
A raccoon struts, so full of pride,
Winking at critters scattered wide.

Morning glories climb and twirl,
In a dance that makes them whirl.
A frog croaks tunes from his pad,
His stage, the muck, but he's not sad.

Hummingbirds take flight in bands,
They pirouette on tiny strands.
A caterpillar's got some sass,
Dreaming of wings, he won't be last.

Fellow critters join the show,
Producing melodies and flow.
Nature's concert, laugh and sway,
Making the most of every day!

Whispers of Wildflower Waking

Whispers rustle through the glade,
As flowers plan their evening parade.
Daisies chuckle with their friends,
  Let's see how this party ends.

Tulips twirl, oh what a sight!
Trying to dance while feeling light.
Poppies bop to their own beat,
  As bees pirouette and greet.

The sun sets low, painting the sky,
  While fireflies blink and pass by.
A sunflower shimmies, can't resist,
"Join the fun, we can't be missed!"

A backdrop of stars begins to gleam,
In this whimsical, wildflower dream.
Laughter lingers, joy takes flight,
  In nature's arms, all feels right!

The Awakening Anthem of the Grove

The trees shake off their winter coats,
Squirrels plotting what to gloat.
Birds return with tunes to sing,
As buds burst forth—oh, what a fling!

Jumps of joy in soft sunlight,
Butterflies dance, oh what a sight!
Critters giggle near the brook,
Nature's mischief in every nook!

The wind whispers ancient jokes,
While flowers sprout in silly folks.
Every whisper brings a laugh,
As trees join in the grand ballet half!

From slumber sweet, all things awake,
Even the acorns start to shake.
In the grove, a merry scene,
Where nature pranks with shades of green!

Echoes of the Quiet Transformation

Once upon a frosty night,
The forest dreamt beyond our sight.
But springs does tease those slumbering trees,
With tickles from a playful breeze!

The rabbits grin with fluffy tails,
As daffodils sport leafy veils.
Old man's beard, the mossy throne,
Whispers secrets to the stone.

A tiny bee in clumsy flight,
Wanders off, takes a funny bite.
The flowers giggle, 'Not so sweet!'
They close up tight on tiny feet!

The sun arrives with a goofy grin,
Sprinkling laughter where buds begin.
Nature chuckles, what a show,
As life erupts in a jubilant flow!

The Renewal of Breath in Silence

Early dawn with yawns, oh dear,
The world wakes up—can you hear?
Moss giggles as the sun awakes,
While frogs in ponds make silly quakes!

Every leaf a jester bright,
Joking about the moonlit night.
The cool breeze mocks the sleeping deer,
And whispers tales for all to hear.

Plants blossom, bowing low,
With winks and grins, a jolly show.
Dancing shadows weave around,
In this stillness, joy is found!

Life returns with frolicsome flair,
Winds of whimsy swirl in the air.
Every tickle brings on a cheer,
As nature revels, year after year!

Frost-Kissed Dreams of Spring

The frosty breath starts to fade,
Old winter's woes—oh, how they've played!
The saplings stretch and make a grin,
With dreams of sun-soaked days to win.

In the soil, worms wiggle delight,
Singing songs to the coming light.
Ladybugs laugh, wearing red,
As raindrops dance on flowerbed!

Chirping crickets start their tease,
While clouds form faces in a breeze.
Nature loves this jolly jest,
Pretending all is one big fest!

As spring bursts forth with jokes in play,
Every creature joins the fray.
Wit and humor in every nook,
As life awakes—come take a look!

Life's Awakening Beneath the Snow

In winter's grasp, we snore and dream,
Yet, in the morn, the sun will beam.
Snowmen pout, with carrot noses,
While squirrels dance in cute little poses.

The shovels sing a funny tune,
While penguins sashay 'neath a silver moon.
Ice cubes chime from mugs of cheer,
As laughter spills loud, far and near.

The trees in white wear gowns so bright,
As giggles soar like birds in flight.
Snowflakes tumble, soft and bold,
While winter tales begin to unfold.

And when the thaw begins to show,
All critters burst from drifts of snow.
With coffee cups and cocoa brims,
Life stirs awake from frosty whims.

Luminous Awakening at Dawn's Gate

The rooster crows with jolly flair,
While sleepy heads all toss and glare.
Morning light, a golden hue,
Chirps a song that's fresh and new.

A cat yawns wide, its belly round,
While coffee brews a joyful sound.
Birds in trees hop, flap, and play,
As breakfast plates hold stacks of fray.

The sun's a clown that jokes and bends,
Painting skies with colorful trends.
Pancakes flip and syrup drips,
As giggles escape from sticky lips.

GoodMornings bounce, as friends all meet,
Over waffles and a treat.
Laughter rings with hearts so bold,
A day of fun begins to unfold.

Whispers of Workers in the Undergrowth

In the glade, ants march with flair,
Marching ants, a tiny air fair.
All around, the critters scurry,
As bees complain, all in a hurry.

The worms wiggle, plotting a scheme,
While ladybugs hitch a ride on a dream.
Garden gnomes stand tall and proud,
Pretending they're chatting with the cloud.

With trowels raised, the squirrels' brigade,
Digging holes for their fresh nut parade.
And flowers bloom, in colors wild,
As nature plays the humble child.

Whispers echo through the trees,
A bustling world at work, oh please!
In the garden, the laughter hums,
As life awakens, what a fun-filled thrum!

Songs of the Shimmering Glade

In shimmering light, the party calls,
Where daisies sway and nature sprawls.
Frogs croak tunes with a ribbit style,
As dragonflies dance for a little while.

Butterflies gossip with haste and glee,
Trading secrets 'round the old oak tree.
Crickets play the night's sweet tune,
While fireflies twinkle, bright as a moon.

The breeze carries giggles, secrets untold,
As acorns drop like little gold.
The glade's alive, a nature's fest,
Where every creature knows it's blessed.

With each heartbeat, a laughter rings,
The forest plays, and the whole world sings.
In this joyful glade, where fun won't end,
Life's vibrant dance will always bend.

Rustling Secrets of the Grove

The trees whisper secrets, oh so sly,
"Did you hear? The squirrels are getting spry!"
Branches rustle with laughter and cheer,
As woodland critters have a dance party near.

The wind plays the flute, a mischievous tune,
While raccoons waltz under a smiling moon.
Leaves giggle softly, they know what to do,
As flowers roll over, laughing anew.

A hare with a top hat hops in delight,
Inviting the frogs for a fancy night.
They sip dewdrops, toast to the fun,
As sunbeams play tag 'till the day is done.

The grove is alive, a circus of glee,
With whispers and chuckles from each leafy tree.
So come join the jest, don't miss the show,
In this quirky kingdom where giggles grow.

Awakening Amber Hues

Golden leaves chuckle, stretching wide,
Flaunting their shades, like it's a pride ride.
With every rustle, a joke's in the air,
Who knew nature could be such a flair?

The sun peeks through with a playful grin,
Tickling the ground where new life begins.
Daffodils dance, all dressed up in gold,
Sharing secrets that never get old.

Bees hum a tune that's simply absurd,
While butterflies flutter, a flippy bird.
Nature's a comedian, who knew this was true?
In a world full of colors, just waiting for you.

Every splash of amber, a giggle indeed,
In this lively canvas, joy is the seed.
So grab a leaf-boat, sail through the hue,
And soak up the laughter that's freshly born, too!

The Song of the Seasonal Shift

As seasons tumble like a jolly old fool,
The trees hum a tune that shimmers like jewels.
Winter's a joker, with ice-cube tricks,
While spring cracks jokes like a bag of old picks.

Birds with their voices like tiny brass bands,
Rehearse for the antics of summer's grand plans.
A stage of bright colors, all eager to play,
While autumn awaits with its leaves on display.

Each breeze brings a punchline, a quirky delight,
As nature argues 'bout who brings the light.
A plant with a giggle, a trunk with a sway,
Sings "I'll see you tomorrow, what fun we'll display!"

In this comedic ballet of leaf and of bark,
Every change brings a laugh, igniting a spark.
So dance with the seasons, don't miss the jest,
In nature's own theater, we're all just guests.

Sunlit Pathways Through the Trees

Beneath the sun, the forest ignites,
With shadows that tango and laugh in the light.
Squirrels in shades, throw acorns with flair,
While rabbits roll over in soft woodland air.

The pathway winds like a silly old snake,
Tickling the toes of the trees by the lake.
Mushrooms in tutus, oh what a sight,
With hedgehogs in hats singing songs of delight.

Each step is a giggle, each turn full of tease,
As pixies play hopscotch beside the tall trees.
The sun pours its gold, melting all woes,
In this enchanting lane where laughter just grows.

So come take a stroll, let your worries unwind,
In sun-dappled pathways, with joy intertwined.
With nature as comrade and giggles in tow,
You'll find it's a journey where happiness flows.

Frosted Breath of Dawn

A frozen sneeze, the trees all shake,
The sun slips in, a giggled wake.
Pinecones tumble, doing a dance,
A squirrel spots them, what a chance!

Frosty frolics in the chill,
The critters scurry, up and down the hill.
A bird trips over its own two feet,
Chirping loudly, 'Oops! That was neat!'

Morning mugs of steaming cheer,
Snowflakes tumble, oh so near.
They land on noses, laugh all day,
In this frosty, funny play!

Sunrise giggles, time to rise,
Nature's laughter fills the skies.
With every step, a joyful sound,
In this whimsical world abound!

Golden Hour Embrace

Oh look, the sun's in a tight squeeze,
With clouds that dance as if to tease.
The shadows stretch, they seem to jest,
While flowers bloom in colors best.

A bear rolls down, who knew bears could spin?
A butterfly flutters, wearing a grin.
The flowers giggle, what a sight!
In golden hues, everything feels right.

A cricket's serenade with silly flair,
Makes the bunnies twirl in midair.
The wind whispers secrets, a cheeky breeze,
Nature chuckles among all the trees.

Each leaf knows how to wiggle and sway,
In this magical dance at the end of the day.
With every chuckle, the dusk arrays,
A funny farewell, in golden rays!

New Life in the Whispering Woods

Tiny sprouts break through the ground,
While sleepy creatures stretch around.
A woodpecker's knocking, oh what a sound,
Each echoing giggle in nature's playground.

A hedgehog rolls, lost in a game,
Chasing a butterfly, shouting its name.
The rabbits leap, their coats so bright,
In the whispering woods, what a delightful sight!

The brook chuckles as it flows,
Tickling stones, teasing grows.
A salamander sliding down a log,
Crowned with dew, oh what a slog!

Every inch of life seems to play,
In this lively wood, come what may.
A chorus of laughter, in leafy frames,
Whispering woods, with delightful games!

Glimmers of Hope in the Breeze

A gust of wind, a playful tease,
Sending leaves off on a breeze.
Sunbeams giggle, tickling the ground,
While clouds play peek-a-boo all around.

A raccoon dances, sways to the jam,
Wearing acorns like a little glam.
The flowers wink in colors bright,
With every flutter, such pure delight.

The sky paints smiles with tones so bold,
Twilight whispers, a tale untold.
A band of fireflies, lighting the way,
Join in the dance of the end of the day.

With each breeze carries laughter's sound,
In every corner, joy is found.
A celebration of life, so sweet and clear,
In shimmering moments that disappear!

Dreams of the Verdant Year

A squirrel in shades, dancing with glee,
Gathering nuts, as spritely as can be.
He plans a party, with acorns and friends,
No chance for boredom, the laughter never ends.

A rabbit hops in, wearing a hat,
He joins the squirrel, saying, "Look at that!"
They've got a playlist of chirps and squeaks,
The whole forest jams, in whimsical peaks.

The trees are chuckling, oh what a sight,
With leaves that shimmer, reflecting the light.
A carpet of grass, the stage for their show,
Join the fun quickly, just follow the glow.

When sunbeams giggle, and shadows play tag,
Nature's a circus, with every fun brag.
So cheers to the folly, the merriment near,
In the heart of the forest, the fun is sincere.

Transforming Roots in the Soil

In the ground they wiggle, a dandelion crew,
Whispering secrets, and planning a coup.
They're pulling some pranks on the stubborn old rock,
Dancing with dirt, in a lively new flock.

The worms wear glasses, surveying their zone,
"Can you see the view?" they tease with a groan.
"Dig deeper!" they shout, with a comical flair,
While the roots roll their eyes, and dance without care.

They throw a big party, under dark soil skies,
With beetles and bugs, all in silly ties.
The compost heap's spinning, a merry-go-round,
Where laughter's the music, and joy's always found.

So next time you ponder a plant in your yard,
Remember the roots, they're happy and hard.
With a tickle of grass, and a wink from a vine,
The ground is a stage, where the silly can shine.

The Promise of New Beginnings

A seed woke up with quite the surprise,
Poked through the dirt, with curious eyes.
"It's time to stretch, to reach for the sun,
Now dance with the breeze, oh, this will be fun!"

With soil on its face, and a grin so wide,
It juggles the raindrops, as they slide.
The worms cheer it on, with a wiggle and twist,
"Leap high, little sprout, don't dare to be missed!"

As spring likes to giggle, the world comes alive,
Each bud on a branch seems ready to thrive.
The flowers paint canvas, with colors so bright,
And the sun gives a nod, saying, "What a delight!"

So here's to the budding, the leaps and the bounds,
With laughter that echoes, in all of the sounds.
New beginnings are friendly, a joke in the air,
Just look all around, excitement is everywhere!

Vibrancy in the Mist

In the morning mist, there's a giggling stream,
It tickles the rocks, and makes them all beam.
A blurry world dances, in hues that delight,
As the dew drops chuckle, sparkling in light.

The flowers wake up, in their pajamas so bright,
Chatting about dreams, from the depth of the night.
A butterfly flutters, with a wink and a dart,
Says, "Let's paint the day, a work of sweet art!"

The fog rolls like laughter, a curtain of fun,
While trees wave their arms, saying, "Join in the run!"
With colors a-jumble, and sounds so sublime,
The day's just unraveled, like a well-spun rhyme.

Nature's a jester, wearing brilliant shades,
In mists full of vibrancy, where joy never fades.
So revel in wonders, the magic we miss,
In each playful moment, find your share of bliss.

www.ingramcontent.com/pod-product-compliance
Lightning Source LLC
Chambersburg PA
CBHW071820160426
43209CB00003B/144